The Urbana Free Library

To renew: call **217-367-4057**
or go to **urbanafreelibrary.org**
and select **My Account**

D1456703

RACHEL'S STORY

A Real-Life Account of Her Journey from Eurasia

Editor: Michelle Hasselius
Production Specialist: Tori Abraham
The illustrations in this book were created digitally.

Picture Window Books are published by Capstone,
1710 Roe Crest Drive, North Mankato, Minnesota 56003
www.mycapstone.com

Library of Congress Cataloging-in-Publication Data
Library of Congress Cataloging-in-Publication data is
available on the Library of Congress website.
ISBN 978-1-5158-1416-0 (library binding)
ISBN 978-1-5158-1420-7 (eBook PDF)

Glossary

appeal (uh-PEEL)—to ask for
a decision made by a court
of law to be changed

detention center
(di-TEN-shuhn SEN-tur)—a
place where people who
have entered a country illegally
are kept for a period of time

foreign (FOR-uhn)—from another country

hostility (hoss-TIL-uh-tee)—a strong hatred or dislike

RACHEL'S STORY

A Real-Life Account of Her Journey from Eurasia

by Andy Glynne

illustrated by Salvador Maldonado

PICTURE WINDOW BOOKS

a capstone imprint

My name is Rachel. This is the story of my journey from Eurasia.

Life was hard in my country. I didn't go to school, because my mom practiced a different religion from most of the other people.

I saw other children around me. They had normal childhoods. They went to school or played outside with their friends. I felt very different from them.

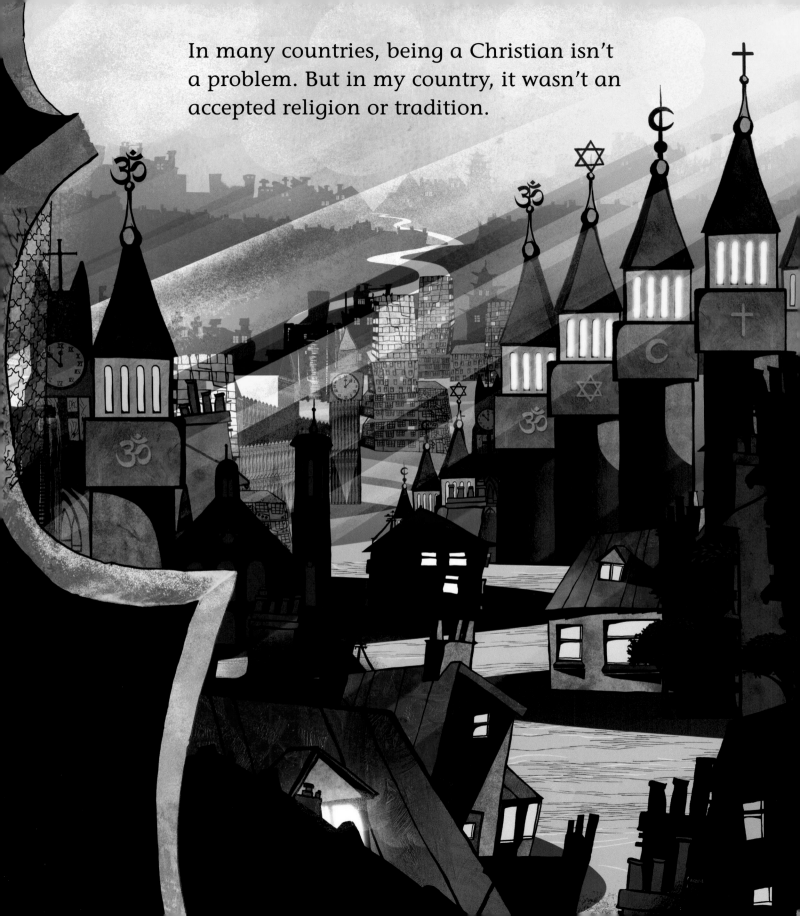

In many countries, being a Christian isn't a problem. But in my country, it wasn't an accepted religion or tradition.

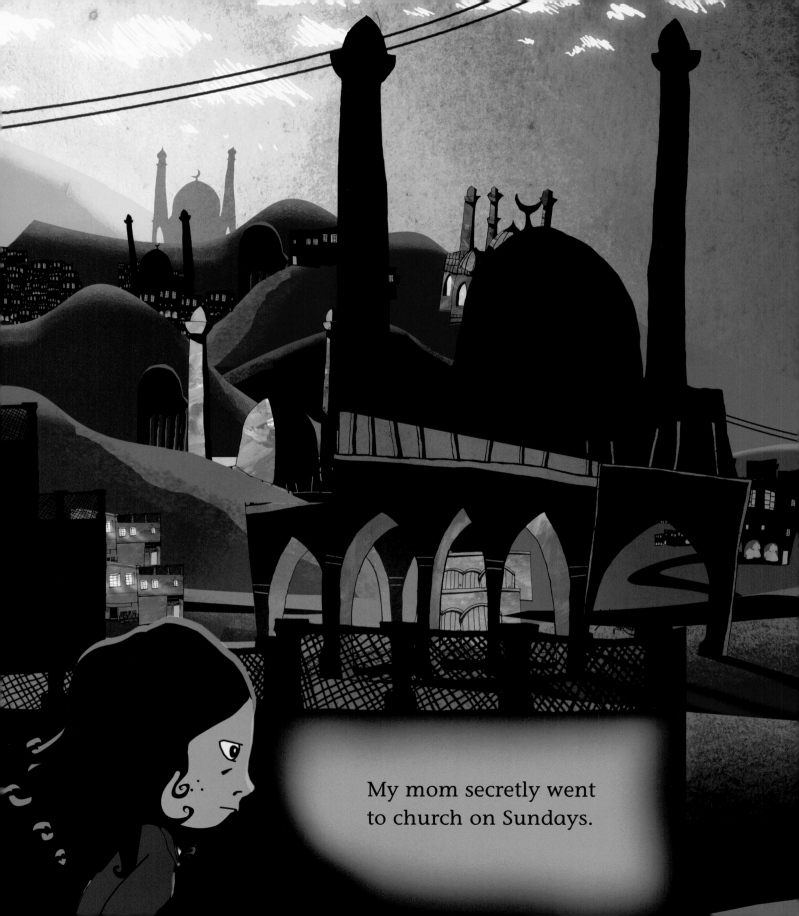

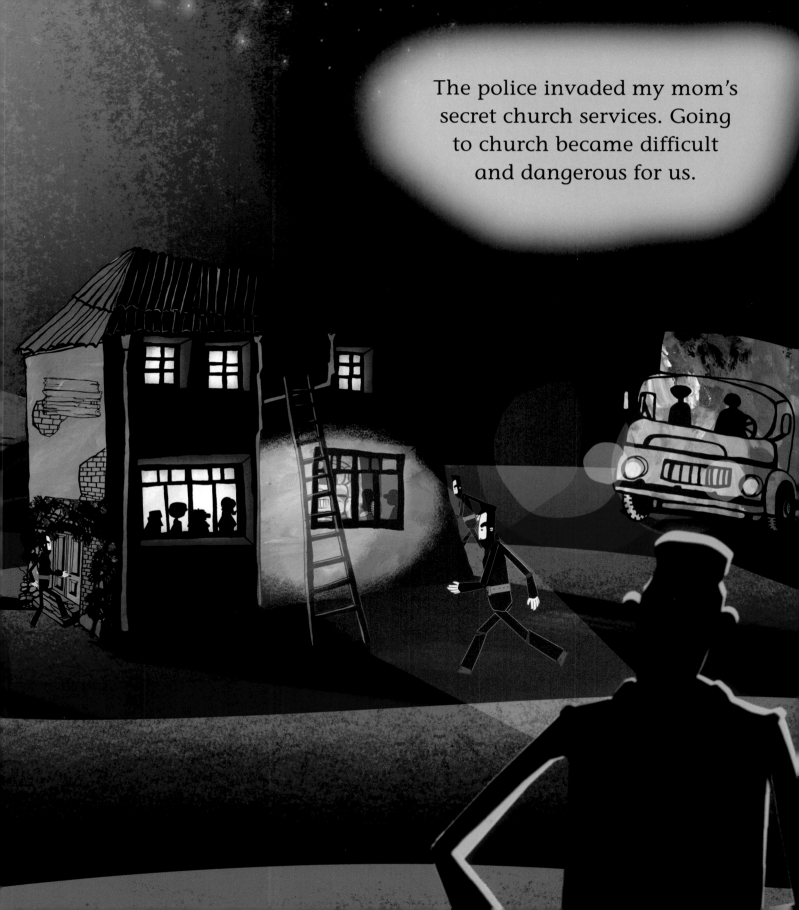

Our lives changed overnight. My mom was treated very badly by people. She wanted to escape.

We secretly decided to leave. We didn't let anyone know. My dad found someone who would take us in the back of a truck.

The three of us clutched each other tightly as we traveled. We slept and slept. It was very dark. We couldn't tell if it was day or night.

We lost track of time. We had
no idea where we were going
or where we would end up.

Eventually we arrived in our new country.
I started to have the kind of childhood
that I had always dreamed of.

I had friends. I could play outside.
We had a normal family life.

Then the letter came that changed everything. Our appeal to remain in the country had been rejected. A single piece of paper had changed my whole life all over again.

At 6 o'clock the next morning, big men came to our house. They looked like huge monsters. They put us in a van and took us to a detention center.

In the detention center, we could hear doors banging all the time. The walls were huge. We couldn't see outside—everything was closed off.

I remember looking up at the high wall. I wished that I could fly over it and escape.

I remember holding the bars in my hands. I couldn't believe that I was stuck in a prison in a foreign country.
I hadn't done anything wrong.

A little while later, we were allowed
to leave the detention center.

I was always afraid that the same
thing would happen again.

And it did.

This time the authorities took us straight to the airport. We were put on a plane and sent back to our home country.

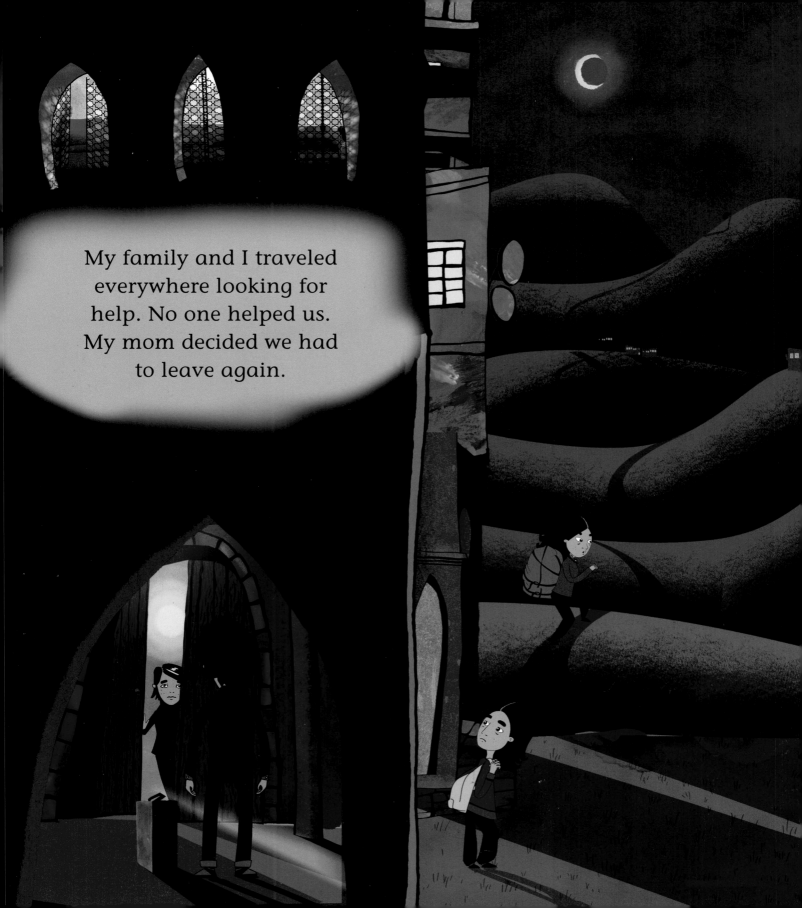

My family and I traveled everywhere looking for help. No one helped us. My mom decided we had to leave again.

My mom found an agent who agreed
to help. We were able to escape.

Back in our new country,
people were very kind and
welcoming. I finally felt safe.

We lived a normal life. But deep down I worried that something horrible could happen at any time.

One day we got a phone call.
I thought it was bad news.
But the lady on the phone
said she had good news.
We were able to stay in
our new country. We
were so happy!

That phone call
changed my whole
life forever!

Lawyer's Office

I've learned from my experience. I've decided that I want to study law. Then I can help people who have the same problems my family and I had.

People are suffering all around the world. When I become an international lawyer, hopefully I can save everyone!